This yearbook belongs to…

....

I HAVE LOVED CREATING MY 2024 YEARBOOK
— I REALLY HOPE YOU ENJOY IT!

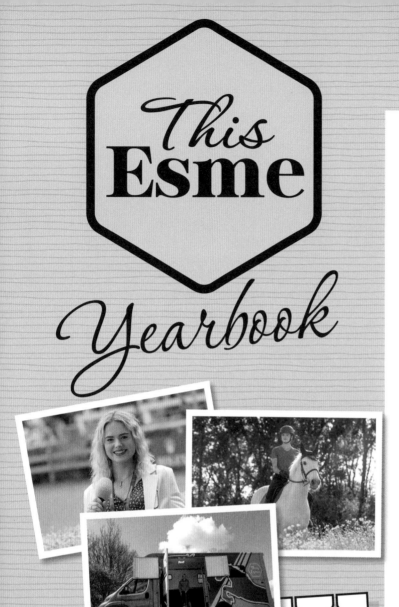

This Esme Yearbook

Published by DJ Murphy (Publishers) Ltd, Olive Studio, Grange Road, Farnham, Surrey GU10 2DQ

WHO DID WHAT IN THIS ESME YEARBOOK 2024

Esme Higgs
Contributors Kiera Boyle, Sarah Burgess, Halima Crabtree, Louise Kittle
Art Editor Paul Smail
Design Lucy Claydon, Adam Witt
Lifestyle photographers Jon Stroud, David Higgs
Images Megan Betteridge, Dean Clarke, Faith Forrest, Ivelin Mitev, Nosyrevy, Irina Shatilova, wabeno, Bjoern Wylezich/shutterstock.com
Managing Director Zoe Cannon
Commercial Director Abi Cannon

This Esme Yearbook is produced under license by DJ Murphy (Publishers) Ltd.
© Copyright DJ Murphy (Publishers) Ltd.

Printed by Printed in Italy by Rotolito S.p.A

ISBN 978-1-913787-18-9

RRP £12.99

Ask me
anything

WILL YOU EVER RIDE DUKE?

Definitely not. Duke is likely to be around 11hh when he finishes growing, so he will be too small for me to ride but I might do some in-hand showing or maybe even carriage driving with him when he's older.

HOW MANY TIMES HAVE YOU FALLEN OFF?

Honestly, it's too many to count! When I first got Casper, he was a very green and nervous horse and I was fairly inexperienced. He used to buck me off two or three times a lesson on a bad day, but I got some help and we haven't looked back since then.

WHAT MADE YOU WANT TO KEEP DONKEYS?

The donkeys have actually been living at the farm since before I was born. They belonged to the old owners of the property who left them behind when they moved. Even though I didn't exactly choose to keep them, I 100% wouldn't be without them!

WILL YOU EVER SELL CASPER?

Never! Casper is a real one of a kind and it takes him a long time to get to know people. Plus, he's getting a bit older now, so it wouldn't be fair to sell him. He's definitely part of the family and you wouldn't sell them – would you?

WHAT MADE YOU WANT TO START RIDING?

I honestly can't remember a time when I didn't want to ride. There was a riding school that used to take groups of children out on hacks past our house and I used to climb on the windowsill to get a better view. As soon as I was old enough, I begged my parents to book me a riding lesson, and then one day I was invited to a horse riding birthday party – it was the best day of my life!

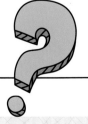

IF YOU COULD GET ANOTHER PET WHAT WOULD IT BE?

I have absolutely fallen in love with Ruby and I really enjoy taking her on long walks, so I think it would have to be a puppy of my own. However, I travel such a lot with work that it wouldn't be fair to have one right now – unless I can talk my parents into looking after them for me whenever I'm away...

A shallow loop is a great exercise to incorporate into your schooling repertoire. It's a good test to check if your pony is listening to you and will help improve his suppleness, too.

Top tip

Shallow loops can be a handy manoeuvre to ride in a busy warm-up arena when you need to move around another competitor, or at home when your arena has a few jumps set up in it.

HOW TO RIDE...
A shallow loop

The start

As I'm riding around the short end of the arena, I look towards the corner marker (F,K,M or H depending on which rein I'm on) and let Joey know I'm about to ask him to do something by riding a half-halt. As I get to the marker, I ask Joey to leave the track and head towards the three-quarter line so that we reach it just before halfway down the arena.

The middle

Before I reach the three-quarter line, I ask Joey to change his bend so that we loop around to head back towards the track. I try to keep him between my new inside leg and outside rein as I ask for the bend, and use my outside leg if he drifts to the outside.

The end

Just before we get to the next corner marker, I ask Joey to change his bend again so that when we return to the track, he's on the correct bend. As we transition from one bend to the other, I use my new inside leg to ask Joey to move over to the outside track and ask him to bend through his whole body, not just with his head and neck.

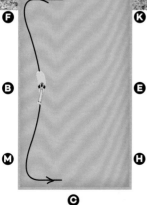

Top tip

Shallow loops can be ridden as 5- or 10-metre loops. If you're riding a 5-metre loop, you'll ride to the three-quarter line, whereas a 10-metre loop goes all the way to the centre line.

Horses and ponies are just as individual as people, so it's important to think about their personalities when you train them.

COMPLEX CASPER

Although Casper has the odd spicy moment, these days he's normally super-chilled

Casper's personality

Even though I've had Casper for years he's still a bit of an enigma at times. He was very head shy when I got him and it took a long time for him to trust me. He's the same with other horses – it's taken over a year for Duke to win him over! But once Casper lets you in, he's such a loving little horse. These days I would take him anywhere, although he'll still surprise me every now and then with a little spook or unscheduled zoomie. He enjoys spending time on his own and doesn't want to be over fussed, but when it's on his terms he will relax and enjoy a good groom and a cuddle.

In the saddle

Casper can be a real potato in the school. It's his way of making it very clear that it's not his favourite thing – yet he's too polite to make a big fuss about it. When it comes to jumping he's a different horse! He really picks himself up and lets me know he's ready for anything. Casper loves hacking, too, and is very happy for the two of us to be out in the countryside for hours.

Casper's week

When I'm planning Casper's exercise and training for the week I try to create a balance of activities to keep his mind happy and his body healthy. Here's a typical week...

MONDAY = DAY OFF

TUESDAY = LONG HACK

WEDNESDAY = FLATWORK

THURSDAY = JUMPING

FRIDAY = DAY OFF

SATURDAY = LONG HACK

SUNDAY = POLEWORK

Making flatwork fun

Flatwork is a really important part of a ridden horse's routine as it gives you the opportunity to give them a good work out and concentrate on any areas of weakness or stiffness. Because Casper isn't mad about going round in circles in the arena, I have to be a bit creative with him. I usually start by doing Casper's warm up on a mini hack. I pop my high-vis on and leap into the saddle for a short wander along the lane and back to give Casper a chance to stretch his legs before we get going in the school. I find it makes *sooo* much difference to how receptive he is to my aids.

When we're in the arena, I don't waste much time before we're trotting and cantering around. Once Casper has had a little canter he's much more forward and wants to listen to every instruction I give him. When he's fully focused, I ask him to make some transitions within the pace – this means I ask him for a collected trot and then a few lengthened strides before asking him back to a working trot again. This kind of work is really good for a horse like Casper who can be a little lazy at times, because it keeps him active, engaged and listening to me.

Active mind, active body

Casper is not the kind of horse you can ride around the arena for hours, so I have to make every second count. Here are some of my favourite exercises for him:

1. Round the clock This fun exercise involves me riding Casper on a 20 metre circle at E. I picture the circle being a clock face, with the points where it crosses the centre line being 12 and six o'clock and the E and B markers being three and nine o'clock. Whenever I reach a different time on my imaginary clock I ride a change of pace. So, for example, I might ask for canter at 12, trot at three, canter again at six and walk at nine.

2. Strides apart In this exercise I ask Casper to shorten or lengthen his strides along the long side of the arena. I like to see how few, or how many, canter strides we can fit in between the F and K markers or the M and C markers.

3. Super loopy I ask Casper to ride a three-loop serpentine like the one on page 30, but this time I ride a small circle after each loop I make.

4. Take a break When you're riding a horse with this level of intensity, you need to give them lots of breaks and let them stretch their neck out long and low.

How to be a
BETTER RIDER

Want to become stronger in the saddle? I've got six things you can practise to help change your riding for the better!

As an avid equestrian, I'm always trying to improve my riding so that I become the best rider I can be for my horses. I enjoy having regular lessons so I can learn as much as possible, and I make sure I exercise often when I'm not on board a horse. Want to know how you can improve your riding skills? Here are my top six tips to try both in the saddle and at home.

1 Stand up in your stirrups

Standing up in your stirrups is a great test of balance and strength. This is something my coach asks me to do as part of my warm up, even though it gives me sore legs afterwards! When you stand up in your stirrups, it automatically puts your lower leg in a strong position so you get that perfect line from shoulder to hip to heel. You might find it hard to maintain at first but keep practising and your muscles will soon build up in the correct places.

2 Video yourself

Asking a friend to video you while you're riding in the arena or having a lesson is a fantastic way to improve your riding. I love being able to look back on my session to see which areas I'll need to focus on more and what parts went well. It can be helpful to view your riding from the ground, especially if your coach is explaining something that you don't quite understand. That way, you can work on it with more clarity next time you ride.

I often use resistance bands when I'm off the horses. They're great to include in pilates sessions because they encourage your muscles to work that little bit harder so you can become even stronger and straighter through your body.

3 Use resistance bands

An incredible tool I love to use when I'm having a lesson is resistance bands. You can get some that are designed especially for riding to help improve rider biomechanics. This is an area of riding I'm really passionate about, and it's great fun to ride with the bands on to help me stay in a perfect position.

4 Practise lateral work

Lateral work is a great workout, not only for your horse, but also for you! Riding lateral movements regularly, such as leg-yield and shoulder-in, is a great way to work on your own straightness in the saddle. You need total control over each of your limbs so they can work independently of each other. These moves also require you to sit central in the saddle so your horse doesn't become crooked.

5 Take up pilates

Practising pilates at home is one of my favourite ways to keep fit for riding. It's popular with lots of top riders because it helps you stay really supple and strong through your core. I like to incorporate an exercise ball, bands and some light weights into my exercise routine, too. Why not see if you can find some pilates classes near you, or look up some equestrian-focused exercises on YouTube for a home workout?

6 Don't forget cardio

Pilates will help you become stronger, but it's important not to forget about your cardio. Running, swimming and cycling are all fantastic ways to improve your endurance levels, and this will pay off when you're in the saddle. Making sure you build things up gradually is the best way to improve your confidence and see improvements without the risk of injury.

As white as SNOW

Grey ponies really stand out from the crowd when they're gleaming white, but they can be a nightmare to keep clean! I've got five handy tips to help keep your grey pony sparkling

16

Tip #1
Rugs, rugs, rugs!

One of my best tips for managing grey ponies is to keep them covered! With the help of rugs, hoods and even tail bags, there are plenty of handy products available that will help keep your horse protected from the dirt. Turning him out in a combo rug in the winter will help keep him as mud-free as possible, and you could pop on a hood if you need him to stay particularly clean for an upcoming competition. In the summer, you can still cover him with a fly sheet or sweet itch rug if you need him to be extra sparkling.

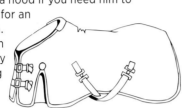

Tip #2
Scrub-a-dub-dub

If your pony comes in covered from head to toe with wet mud, washing him off may be the only option! Using warm water if you can, rinse off the mud and dirt with the hose at a gentle pressure. If you're heading to a competition and you need your pony to be super-clean, enlisting the help of some purple shampoo could be just the thing! The purple colour helps to counteract the yellow in stains to leave your horse's body and tail and bright as can be.

> **Did you know?**
> It's always better to let the mud dry and brush it off later if you can. This is because washing your horse too often can weaken his skin and remove some of the natural oils from his coat.

Tip #3
Brush it off

Sometimes your horse might be covered in huge clumps of mud! If you need to do a full body groom, there are a few excellent grooming tools you simply have to try! My top three pieces of kit are a...

- **magic brush** These handy little plastic brushes can tackle almost anything. They are great for destroying muddy patches and my horses seem to think they are having a massage at the same time!
- **dandy brush** A classic! Nothing beats a good old-fashioned dandy brush. The thick bristles are excellent for flicking away big clumps of dirt
- **cactus cloth** The perfect tool to remove mud from sensitive areas, such as your horse's head and legs. It's also great for giving your horse a once over when most of the dirt has gone

Tip #4
Super spray

There are numerous lotions and potions designed to help keep your grey horse gleaming, and I go through lots of bottles owning four! I love to use conditioner in manes and tails because, not only does it make my ponies easier to brush, but it also helps the dirt slide right off when they're in the field! Another handy tip is to put baby oil on your horse's white legs in winter for the same effect.

> **Did you know?**
> You can buy refill bottles and recycle them to help the environment and reduce waste if you go through a lot of spray like I do!

Tip #5
Goodbye stains

Grey ponies are notorious for getting themselves covered in yellow and green stains! The dirt just loves to cling to their white hair, whether they're having a good roll in the field or a sleepy lie down in their stable. My go-to piece of kit is stain remover spray. All you have to do is spray it onto the stain, wait a few seconds, then groom or sponge it off. Voila! The stain has vanished. It's a total game changer and I couldn't live without it.

Duke's
A-MAZE-ING POLES

Introducing Duke to poles in a fun, low-pressured way

The set up

This pole layout is really quick and simple to set up and only requires six poles. Position four poles so they overlap the centre line by one coloured section alternately as shown. Then position one pole on each side to form two open squares.

Before you start

Normally when you work a pony over poles, you warm up his muscles to avoid injury. With Duke, it's more about warming up his mind. As I take him into the arena, it's so important I give him time to take in his environment and let him explore the poles at his own pace. I look for body language cues that tell me Duke is relaxed and ready to learn something new – like a deep sigh, soft, relaxed ears and lowering of his head and neck. It doesn't matter how long it takes for him to reach this point, training Duke is all about positive experiences and having fun.

Baby steps

Before I tackle the whole exercise, I introduce Duke to the poles slowly by walking him between two poles and out over the single pole at the end. This gets him used to staying within the poles but doesn't ask too much of him. When he does this successfully, Duke gets a neck scratch and lots of praise!

Learning labyrinth

Duke's challenge is to walk through the maze of poles. He needs clear instruction from me to turn left and right as we wiggle through the poles. If I think he's getting confused or feeling unsure of himself, I ask him to halt and I give him plenty of reassurance. Duke's a pony who loves exploring new things, so he soon gets the hang of it and looks pretty pleased with himself.

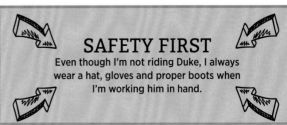

SAFETY FIRST

Even though I'm not riding Duke, I always wear a hat, gloves and proper boots when I'm working him in hand.

GROW YOUR OWN
CARROTS

Now I have my own garden, I couldn't resist growing something special for the equines to enjoy, too!

WHAT YOU'LL NEED:

- a small patch of garden or containers for planting and some compost
- trowel
- rake
- carrot seeds
- watering can

1 Prepare the soil by removing any weeds and loosening the earth to a depth of around 15cm using your trowel. Then rake over the area until it's flat and even. If you are planting your carrots in containers, fill them with compost, leaving a 3–4cm gap at the top.

2 Make a small trench for your seeds. This only needs to be around 5mm deep. Sprinkle the seeds thinly along the trench – dropping a couple of seeds every centimetre. Gently cover the seeds with soil before watering them.

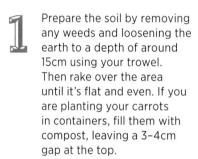

Top tip

Caracas is a good variety of carrot for growing in small containers.

3 If the weather is dry, water your seeds every couple of days during the germination period. After three weeks, you should start to see little seedlings popping up. Most varieties take around 10 weeks before the carrots are ready to harvest, but check them every few days to see if they need water.

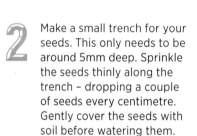

Top tip

Sow your carrot seeds between March and July.

4 After 10 weeks, it's time to harvest your carrots by taking hold of them at the base of the plant and pulling the carrots up out of the ground. Give them a quick wash and they're ready for you or your pony to eat!

A DAY IN THE LIFE OF
Joey

As my competition horse, we're bound to spend the most time together

A DAY IN
THE LIFE

7.00 AM

He might not look it, but Joey is actually quite a foodie and I think all hell would break out if he weren't the first to be fed in the mornings. Luckily for him, he's right next door to the feed room, so he doesn't ever have to wait long for his breakfast. I leave him in peace while he demolishes his food – which gives me time to feed the others.

7.30 AM

Joey heads out to his field - but not until Casper has made sure there aren't any lions waiting to eat him! Although Joey dominates in the field, he's a young horse and he still isn't totally sure about being turned out without his buddies. Once he's got someone to hang out with, he's straight off to his paddock.

HEADING OUT FOR A LESSON

2.00 PM

I often train Joey away from home with great instructors like Felicity and Dee. It's a short trip on the horsebox but it's worth it for the amazing facilities and the fantastic help that we receive. I pop my tack in the horsebox and, with his boots and tail guard on, Joey is ready to roll. When he arrives, he knows exactly where he is and it's not long before I'm tacked up and on board ready for our lesson.

3.00 PM

Today we're jumping and I have my work cut out for me as Dee is putting us through our paces. But before I can even go over a cross-pole, I have to make sure I have Joey in a good-quality canter and that my position is spot on!

Dee brings her iPad along so that she can show me exactly what we're doing right and wrong. Even though I feel like I'm on camera all the time, it's amazing how much she picks up on and how much I can learn from watching it back. We have a great session and my head is full of things I want to work on and exercises I want to remember.

Once we've finished training, I give Joey a long cool down and a lovely stretch so he's ready to go back on the horsebox for the short trip home.

LOOKING SUPER-SMART!

4.30 PM

I take Joey off the box, offer him a drink and then turn him back out into the field for a leg stretch before tea time. Every time Joey arrives home, he does a huge whinny – so I know he's pleased to see his pals.

6.00 PM

Once Joey and Casper are in from the field, it's time for Joey's stretches. He gets a treat for doing them, so he's always super-happy to give them a go. Next, it's teatime – and also time to tuck Jo-Jo up in his stable for the night.

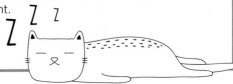

GRAND
plans

Running a yard of four horses takes lots of planning and organisation! Find out how I manage everything from dawn 'til dusk

You all know that I love to be organised, and that's the only way I'm able to juggle all four of my horses! With my trusty planner to hand, I create easy-to-follow daily, weekly and annual routines and keep track of all the details in my horses' lives so I can take the best possible care of them. From exercising to feeding, here's how I plan my perfect yard life.

Daily feeding routines

As all my horses have very different needs when it comes to their diets, I make sure each one has a bespoke feeding regime. I like to allocate a bucket colour to each of them so I can remember whose feed is whose! Luckily, I know each horse's feed from memory by now, but it can be really useful to write down on a blackboard in the feed room what each one has. That way, if anyone else has to feed them for any reason, all the information they need is right there!

Joey's at the top of pecking order, so is always fed first when the horses are stabled, otherwise he gets a bit hangry! Then I work my way along from Casper to Mickey to Duke. I can't forget the donkeys, of course, so after the horses have been fed, I head out to the field to give them their buckets.

Weekly exercise routines

I like to make sure all my horses have plenty of exercise so they can stay as fit and healthy as possible! However, they all have very different exercise requirements, so I have to tailor their fitness plans to suit them. It helps to keep a table of each horse's workload week by week, which I store in my planner so I can co-ordinate my time and ensure they all have an equal amount of love and attention.

For example, I try to make sure Joey and Casper have at least one hack a week, and I vary their work as much as I can by including in their regimes a mixture of flatwork, polework, lungeing and jumping. For Mickey and Duke, who are not ridden, I plan time to take them for fun walks in hand around the countryside and I also teach them adorable tricks in the arena to help keep their brains active and to strengthen our bonds.

Annual field rotation

I like to turn the horses out in pairs, with Joey and Casper in a field together and Mickey and Duke together. This is because Joey and Casper are in harder work so they can have a bit more grass, whereas Mickey and Duke are much smaller and aren't in full work, so need to be kept on restricted grass! It's important to make sure the paddocks stay in tip-top condition, so I tend to rotate them throughout the seasons.

In the winter, Joey and Casper go into separate fields at the back of the yard, where they have plenty of grass to keep them happy. Plus, there's more space, so it doesn't matter as much if the ground gets a bit muddy! Mickey and Duke are very close by, but they have less grass to ensure they don't get too fat! When spring rolls around, I move the horses into fresh paddocks. This allows the winter fields to have a rest, ready to be rolled and re-seeded before they're used again the following year.

Managing appointments

I try to make my life easy and schedule my horses' appointments at the same time, if I can. That way, there's no confusion as to who is having what! Plus, it helps to save on callout fees, too. My horses all have the farrier at the same time, and I try to align their vaccinations and teeth so that they happen all together. If one horse needs a visit from the saddle fitter or physio more often, then I'll schedule that in separately, but I make sure to write it onto my calendar that I keep at the yard. I also set up a notification on my phone so I don't forget, and of course add it into my planner!

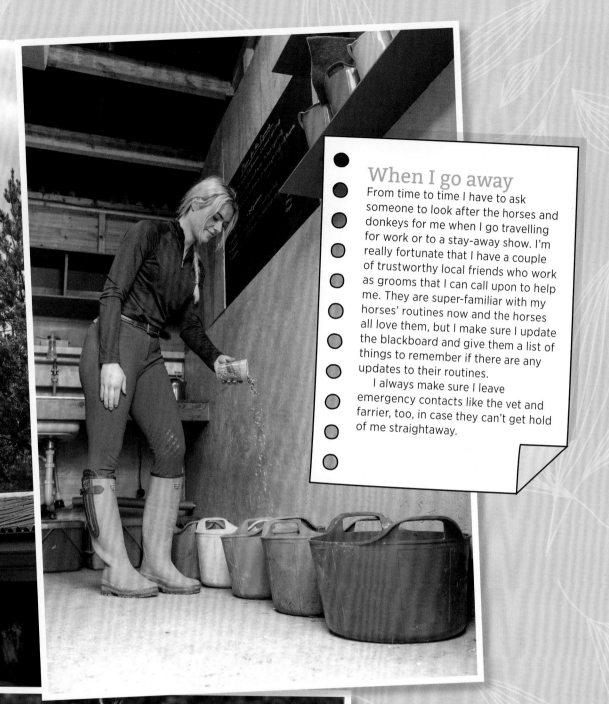

When I go away

From time to time I have to ask someone to look after the horses and donkeys for me when I go travelling for work or to a stay-away show. I'm really fortunate that I have a couple of trustworthy local friends who work as grooms that I can call upon to help me. They are super-familiar with my horses' routines now and the horses all love them, but I make sure I update the blackboard and give them a list of things to remember if there are any updates to their routines.

I always make sure I leave emergency contacts like the vet and farrier, too, in case they can't get hold of me straightaway.

Using a planner

One of the most valuable tools I always use to help me keep track of all my horses is a daily planner! In one of these special books, I can log absolutely everything I need to remember, including a calendar to keep track of each horse's appointments, notes about their diet and health as well as scheduling in lessons and fitness plans for each of them. I'd totally recommend using a planner, whether you own one horse, ten horses or even none! They can still come in handy for all aspects of life, including school and riding lessons!

REDUCE, REUSE, RECYCLE!

Putting the planet first is so important to me

Fuelled by electric

I love living so close the horses. It means I don't spend hours driving to and from the yard, which is much better for the environment. But sometimes there's just no getting away from travelling – such as when I'm heading to a meet-up or visiting a famous rider. To minimise the impact these journeys have, I chose an electric car that I charge at the stables using the power generated from our solar panels. Sometimes it can take a bit longer to get where I need to go, as I may need to charge up halfway through a journey, but this gives me chance to grab a coffee and reply to a few your comments.

Something old something new

You guys know I love a good DIY project and upcycling is my favourite thing of all. Bringing the dressers and cabinets for my tack room back to life was seriously satisfying and I absolutely love the final look. When you make use of something old instead of buying something new, you're making a choice that will help sustain our planet for generations to come. Now I've moved into the cottage, I'm looking forward to more projects like this – so watch this space!

Rehoming

Part of my job involves working with brands to showcase their products, so I end up with a large amount of stuff! Each horse only needs so many rugs and boots, so I like to give away the equipment and clothing I don't need to the horse charities I work closely with. It means things don't go to waste, as the charity can put them to good use – and it saves them money, too.

What goes around comes around

I probably spend around an hour every day mucking out – and when you spend that long mucking out, you end up with a lot of manure! By carefully stacking and stepping the muck heap, it starts to rot down. After three to six months, the manure will be fully composted and can be used on the garden – so I stick it in a wheelbarrow and take it to my grandparents to use on their veg patch.

The problem with packaging

With some of the products I use for the horses, there's just no getting away from plastic packaging – such as haylage, which must be kept sealed away from oxygen. I choose Silvermoor haylage, as they're committed to making their products as sustainable as possible and only use 100% recyclable polythene packaging for their haylage. They also use fully recyclable paper packaging for their new stable treats.

Did you know?
A horse can produce up to eight tonnes of manure a year!

The serpentine snakes its way down the arena in one fluid movement, but you can break it down into little chunks to make it easier for you and your pony to learn. Find out how I train for the perfect serpentine.

HOW TO RIDE...
A serpentine

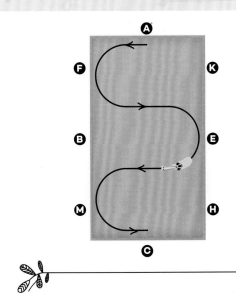

The start

Although this movement normally starts from the centre line marker, you actually need to continue on the track for about four metres – one or two strides – before starting your first loop. I'm riding Joey on the left rein at the start of my serpentine, so I ask him to leave the track and ride half a circle to the left before riding two or three straight strides across the centre line.

The middle

As I cross the centre line, I change my diagonal and ask Joey to pick up the right bend. Then I ask him for another half circle – this time going to the right. As soon as I start the circle, my eyes are on the point where I think it should end. At the end of the half circle, I look straight ahead and ask Joey to straighten his body. Then I ride forwards for two or three strides.

The end

This time when I cross the centre line, I change Joey's bend to the left and adjust my diagonal again. After our two or three straight strides, we make our final half circle. This time, my eyes are fixed on a point on the track roughly four metres from the C marker where my half circle should finish. At the end of the final loop, I ride straight on the track for a couple of strides before we get to C.

It's all about the maths!

In a 20x40 metre arena, each loop of a three-loop serpentine is a half circle just over 13 metres in diameter with two or three straight strides across the centre line before the next loop.

home
AWAY FROM
home

Join me on a sleepover adventure with Joey in tow!

Have you ever camped overnight with your pony? Well, I can tell you, it's the best fun ever! Whether you're attending Pony Club camp, training or staying away at a show, you're guaranteed to have the best time. Not sure what to expect? I've kept a diary of what I get up to at a sleep-away camp with Joey, so you can get a feel for what it entails!

→→

HOME

adventure

9:00AM ARRIVING →→

I arrive at camp in good time. I want to make sure I'm not rushing and that I can nab a good spot to park the horsebox in! I leave Jo-Jo on the box munching his haynet while I head straight to his temporary stable so I can lay a shavings bed, hang his haynet and source some water for his bucket. Once my mucking out tools are stowed away, I lead Joey over and get him settled in his comfy new stable for the weekend.

9:30AM SETTING UP CAMP

Once Joey's sorted, it's time to turn my attention to my own sleeping quarters. I fully sweep out the horse area so it feels more homely. Then, I put up the little table in the living area and organise my luggage in the wardrobe. That way, I can easily grab what I need. If there's anything else to transport to the stables, I pop it in my wheelbarrow and take it over for easy access.

Top tip

When you're packing for camp, there's a lot to take, especially when you have to pack for your pony as well as yourself! I find it helps to make a checklist you can refer to along the way, so you don't forget anything!

10:00AM FIRST RIDING SESSION

I need to make sure Joey's tacked up and ready for the first riding session of camp. This is usually flatwork to get us eased in gently. Besides getting his stable and my horsebox set up for camp, I need to make sure we're ready in time for the riding section! I like to keep my tack with me locked away in the horsebox, so I find it easier to lead Joey over to the box to tack up rather than hauling it all the way to the stable block!

12:00PM LUNCH

Once we've completed our flatwork session, it's time for lunch! I'm usually starving by now, so I pop Joey back in his stable to have a rest and a haynet while I tuck into my sandwich! Now's a good time to finish any unpacking. It's not long before I need to get ready for the second riding session of the day.

1:00PM SECOND RIDING LESSON

I love camp so much because there's loads of riding involved! That's why it's super-important that your pony's fit enough to cope with the workload. The second riding session of the day is jumping, and my group get to go cross-country! I have to make sure Joey's kitted out properly and that I'm ready in time to give him a good warm-up before the session starts.

3:00PM CHILL TIME

Tired from all that riding, it's time to chill out with friends and finish setting up camp before dinner time. Camp's a great place to make new friends because everyone's in the same boat and, of course, loves ponies! We have a snack in the lounge and watch some episodes of our favourite show on the iPad. Then I skip out Joey's stable and give him a good groom. If we're lucky, we might even have the chance to listen to a special guest speaker, like a nutritionist or behaviourist, to learn something new while we're waiting for dinner to be ready.

5:00PM DINNER TIME

We usually have a barbecue for dinner at camp and it's always delicious! I take my own plate, knife and fork with me and I have to wash up after dinner. Our meal is always followed by a fun game or a group activity that gets us all out of our seats and laughing the night away!

8:00PM FINAL CHECKS

My friends and I chat and start to wind down for the night, but not without giving our ponies a final check over! We give them their feeds, top up their haynets and water and put on appropriate rugs, along with doing another skip out. There's something super-cosy about mucking out in your PJs!

10:00PM READY FOR BED

Once the ponies are happy, we head back to the horseboxes to get ourselves ready for bed. It's been a long day and I'm more than happy to hit the hay! I brush my teeth and make my bed for the night. I might watch something on YouTube or read a book by torchlight to help me sleep, but it doesn't take me long to drift off. I need to be rested to be ready to do it all again tomorrow!

REELS VS REALITY

My photoshoot fails and the truth behind the lens

When you work with horses like I do, things don't to go to plan 100% of the time – but that's part of what makes it such good fun. Here, I show you a few of the goings on behind the camera.

PHOTOSHOOT READY

DEFINITELY NOT PHOTO READY!

DUKE DESTROYING THE NEW THING AND FRIGHTENING HIMSELF IN THE PROCESS!

DUKE DEMONSTRATING HOW HORSES INVESTIGATE NEW THINGS

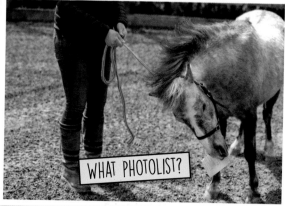

THEY SAID... WE'D LIKE A LOVELY PHOTO OF YOU SMILING AND FEEDING MICKEY A CARROT, MICKEY SAID... DID SOMEONE SAY CARROT?

WHAT PHOTOLIST?

All my horses have such different personalities, so it's really important I don't try to train them in the same way.

JOVIAL JOEY

Joey literally thinks he's a dog. He has such a happy, bouncy personality – I'm amazed he hasn't tried to come in the house!

Joey's personality

There are two sides to Joey's personality. For 95% of the time he's super-chilled, really laid back and lots of fun. However, 5% of the time he has a tendency to be a little bit of a worrier. He doesn't like it when the other horses go off without him – he definitely thinks he's the most important one and should be with me at all times! He thinks he's the boss unless there's something scary and he needs to hide behind Casper. And when I'm away, he likes to pretend he's a highly-strung racehorse instead of the puppy dog you all know and love. Basically he's still quite young, and likes to have the people and things he knows around him for comfort.

In the saddle

Joey is known for putting in 80% effort most of the time. However, when it really counts he's always got 110% for me – like when we're jumping a big course of showjumps, or we head down the centre line at the start of a dressage test. Joey just seems to know when to turn it on, and when he can chillax. The only problem is, I need to learn to ride both Joeys!

Joey's week

I try to create a balance of activities to fill Joey's week. Because he's a competition horse, I work him a little bit harder than Casper, and spend more time in the arena. Here's a typical week...

MONDAY = LONG HACK
TUESDAY = FLATWORK
WEDNESDAY = POLEWORK
THURSDAY = JUMPING
FRIDAY = DAY OFF
SATURDAY = HACK
SUNDAY = FLATWORK

The best start

I find that I get the best out of Joey when he's totally ready to focus on his work. His favourite time to be ridden is in the morning when there are no distractions around. Before I tack Joey up, I put the solarium on for 10–15 minutes to warm up his muscles. It's a real luxury, but I honestly feel the difference in him – both in terms of his body, which feels looser, and his mind, which seems to have improved concentration. After this, I tack him up and continue with the theme of loosening and stretching him so that when I pick up the reins, he's ready to knuckle down and have a great session.

As with many other horses, canter is the key to success with Joey. As soon as he's warmed up sufficiently, I give him a canter around the arena in a light seat. When I bring him back to a trot he feels much more forward! I do this on both reins and then move onto some lateral work, which is great for making your horse or pony more supple. I will often ride through an exercise once in walk before moving up to trot. I do this so that Joey understands what I'm asking him to do. Once he's got the idea, I like to work him in trot and canter so that he stays in an active rhythm.

Straight and supple

I find the key to riding a big horse like Joey is to make sure he's straight and supple. Here are some of my favourite exercises for him:

1. Long and low Every session I do with Joey will start and finish with some long and low work. I ask him to stretch out his head and neck so that his nose is reaching forwards and down towards the arena rubber. Even though he's on a long rein, it's important that he isn't just bumbling along doing his own thing. I put my leg on so that Joey lifts his tummy and I can feel him engage his core and start to swing through his back.

2. Leg yield I like to ride this exercise with a twist. Instead of always turning onto the centre line and asking Joey to step sideways towards the fence, I ride down the long side of the arena and change his bend to the outside. Then I use my new inside leg to ask Joey to step sideways towards the centre line. Riding a mixture of the two really keeps Joey on his toes!

3. Super circles On a 20m circle, I ask Joey to alternate between shoulder-in on the circle – with his forehand tracking on the inside line – and being straight – with his hindlegs following the path of his fronts.

Esme on tour

Find out all my favourite things to do when I'm on the road

As a YouTuber, a big part of my job is touring around the UK and abroad to meet all of you! I absolutely love meeting my fans and visiting some of the amazing venues the equestrian world has to offer, but it's hard work staying on top form after spending a long time travelling! So, I have a few favourite things that help me feel and look great when I arrive at my destination.

HAND LUGGAGE PACKING LIST:

- headphones
- makeup bag
- book to read
- phone charger
- travel mirror
- sun cream
- change of clothes
- laptop
- vlogging camera
- hair brush
- sunglasses
- toothbrush

What's in my makeup bag?

I always like to be able to touch up my makeup so I can look full glam when I'm out and about! I don't tend to wear too much makeup day to day, but when I'm due to go to a meet and greet, I always carry a compact with face powder so I can have a quick glow up after a long journey. Plus, I'm never caught without my fave lip gloss because my lips can get a bit dry when I'm spending a lot of time outside.

TAKING MY FAVOURITE BOOK ALONG WITH ME IS A MUST WHEN I'M ON MY TRAVELS. I'M ALWAYS READING AND HAVE A DIFFERENT NOVEL ON THE GO ALL THE TIME. I PREFER TO READ FICTION WHEN I'M TRAVELLING SO I CAN GET LOST IN ANOTHER WORLD!

There's lots of horsey fiction available to read

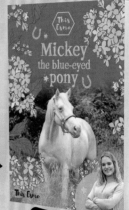

I love to have something great to listen to that can keep me entertained when I'm on the road. Aside from listening to my favourite songs, I absolutely love podcasts. There are so many to choose from on different topics, but I especially love horse-themed ones, so I can learn as much as I can!

WHY NOT CHECK OUT MY PODCAST?

Check-in time

When I arrive at my accommodation, I always like to check out the view from my room first – if it's not night time, that is! Then, I put my bathroom items in their rightful place and hang up my clothes in the wardrobe. I often can't resist flopping onto the bed to test how comfy it is, and if I've had a long journey, I might catch 40 winks before heading off in search of something to eat!

I GO FOR THE LESS IS MORE APPROACH!

Joey's
PROPRIOCEPTION POLES

Next-level lines to improve Joey's body awareness

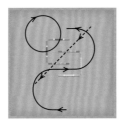

Cool curves

In this exercise I ride an arc through the corner of my layout while riding Joey on a circle. It's really important that I ride a good line in over the middle of the first pole when I'm trotting to give Joey enough room to take a step before heading out over the middle section of the second pole. If I go too wide, the distance will be too long for Joey's stride and if I go too tight to the corner he won't have enough room.

It can be tempting to approach the first pole at a right angle – as we're always taught to ride straight to poles – but in this instance the pole will be at a slight angle as you follow the curve of your circle over the two poles. This exercise can be ridden in walk, too – but you need to ride closer to the corner so that it's a comfortable walk stride for your horse or pony.

Riding a circle over the poles helps Joey bend correctly through his body from his pole all the way to his tail.

Guide rails

This time I'm riding a figure of eight with a change of bend over X. Using the poles as a channel makes me ride straight as I cross the centre line before picking up the new bend and riding out over the pole. This exercise looks easy, but is harder than you think. Stick at it though, because it will really improve your accuracy.

Daring diagonals

This is the hardest line in this layout and I have to think carefully about which poles I'm aiming at. The diagonal line goes over the two middle poles – green in my case – and you need to cross them at a 45° angle, which feels strange. I can feel Joey concentrating as hard as I am as he looks for his next pole and adjusts his stride to fit.

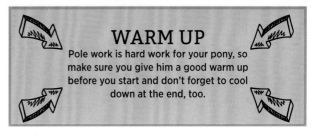

WARM UP

Pole work is hard work for your pony, so make sure you give him a good warm up before you start and don't forget to cool down at the end, too.

IT'S
playtime

From time to time, I set up an obstacle course for the horses. It's great fun and actually teaches the horses and me a surprising amount!

All abord?

Just like the polework layouts I set up, the obstacle courses I build in the arena will work for all the ponies – whether they are ridden or not. Today, I'm working with Duke, so it's all going to be done in hand – but even if your pony is ridden, it's useful to work them in hand from time to time, as it really helps strengthen your bond and gives him a break from school work.

Doing obstacle courses with Duke helps desensitise him to strange-looking objects and funny noises. It helps me to spot when he's not entirely focused on what I'm asking him to do and improves how responsive he is to my aids when I ask him to walk, halt and move away from me. Obstacle courses are also a lot of fun and Duke always gets super-excited when he sees all his toys out in the arena.

Top tip

The closer the cones are to each other, the harder it is to bend around them, so give yourself plenty of space when you begin.

Safety first

Always wear a current-standard safety helmet, gloves and boots when working a horse in hand.

Super slalom

This is a next-level version of a traditional bending race. Instead of just weaving in and out of cones in one line, you need to traverse the course so that you go around the cones on each side alternately as in the diagram. This is quite a challenge for Duke and I can see if he's listening to my body language and changing direction when asked.

I walk on the left-hand side of Duke and try to stay by his shoulder – but it can be quite tricky because he's so small! The idea is not to push and pull him around the cones, as, instead, I want him to move away from me when I give him the signal to bend around to the right and follow me when we are turning to the left. Just as when you're riding, it's really important to look where you want to go. This turns your shoulders in the direction you're heading and makes it clear to your pony what you're asking him to do.

Slip rail

This might look like a little jump, but I'm actually using it as a slip rail. If you ever compete in a Pony Club tetrathlon competition, you'll come across a slip rail on your cross-country round. It's an obstacle for which you dismount, then slide the top rail of the fence out of its bracket and lower one end of it to the floor to allow your pony to walk over it. In my home-made version, I'm going to lower one end of the jump so that Duke and I can walk over it before putting the pole back up. It's really good for Duke to learn to stand patiently while I do something like adjusting the pole – and it will be really handy for you to teach your ponies to stand, too, in case you need to put a jump back up, or raise or lower the course.

Once one end is on the ground, it's time to lead Duke over the pole. Ideally, I want him to step over – not jump – the poles. Sometimes Duke has other ideas about this, but by staying calm and repeating the exercise, he soon learns what I'm looking for and I give him lots of praise so he knows how good he's been. Next, it's time to put the pole back up. This can be tricky as your pony might be eying up the jump, but ask him to stand while you put the pole back on its cup and always reward him with a little neck scratch or stroke when he's done as you asked.

Going for Goal

Some horses love having a ball to play with – and Duke is definitely one of them! It gives him an outlet for his playful behaviour and as Mickey gets older, it will become more and more important that Duke finds his own ways to let off steam. He likes to explore it with his mouth, kick it and occasionally give it a good headbutt! This ball is a specialist equine ball so that no matter how much Duke tries to hurl it around, it will stay in one piece.

Check out page 54 to see the ridden exercises I do with Casper.

Baby steps

Duke's still young, so it's important to keep his sessions short and positive. Tackling too many new obstacles in one go could be too much for him to deal with mentally, so limiting what I ask of him makes sure he has lots of fun and always wants to do more.

MUCKING OUT PLAYLIST

What I'm listening to while I'm working on the yard

SEVENTEEN GOING UNDER
Sam Fender

LITTLE BIT OF LOVE
Tom Grennan

STRESSED OUT
Twenty One Pilots

CHANDELIER
Sia

STRANGERS
Sigrid

BREAK MY SOUL
Beyoncé

LATE NIGHT TALKING
Harry Styles

LOVE STORY
Taylor Swift

ONE KISS
Calvin Harris and Dua Lipa

PUMPED UP KICKS
Foster the People

This **Esme**

A DAY IN THE LIFE OF
Casper

Living the life of an equestrian super-star!

A DAY IN
THE LIFE

7.00 AM

It's a big day for Casper, so as soon as he's finished eating his breakfast, I turn him out in his paddock so he can chill for a while. He's super-chuffed to get out before the others and does a little squeak as he trots the length of the field with his tail in the air!

9.00 AM

After some chill-time in the field, I bring Casper in and tie him up in the wash bay. Today we've got a catalogue photoshoot and he needs to be whiter than white. With my purple shampoo at the ready, I clean Casper from head to toe while he munches on some haylage. With the option of warm water and a solarium to dry him off, Casper thinks he's in heaven!

SOMETIMES I QUESTION
MY LOVE OF GREYS!

11.00 AM

Once Casper is completely dry and gleaming white, it's time to prepare him to travel. Today's photoshoot takes place in one of Casper's favourite places – a wonderful wide-open field where he can gallop until his heart's content. Luckily, it's just a short drive in the horsebox, so with his travel boots on and his gleaming white tail carefully wrapped in a tail bag and guard, we're on our way to the photoshoot.

12 NOON

Our photoshoots often take place in the middle of the day when the light is at its best and there are no time pressures to be finished before it becomes dark. We always make it fun for Casper, so he doesn't even realise he's working. We break up the static shots with long walks through the countryside while we scope out new locations and obviously Casper gets to enjoy some zoomies, too!

The only real difference between a photoshoot and a fun hack is that I try my best to avoid any mud or puddles until we know we've got some great shots. Once we've got the photos we need, I make the most of the location by taking Casper for a fun ride until it's time to take him back to the stables.

NOTHING'S BETTER THAN CLEAN
PONIES AND CLEAN TACK!

2.00 PM

I put Casper back in his paddock as soon as we get back and he usually undoes all my cleaning efforts within 10 seconds of me taking his headcollar off! Next, he makes a beeline for Joey to say hi!

6.00 PM

After a long afternoon in the field, Casper comes into his stable for his dinner and a haynet. He's worked hard today and been a brilliant boy, so I can't help spoiling him with a few treats and cuddles.

"I'M SO LUCKY TO HAVE THE HORSE OF MY DREAMS"

This
Esme

ULTIMATE
obstacles

Casper loves having fun things to think about and challenge him in the school

Fun and games

I like to take inspiration from some of the classic mounted games races when I build an obstacle course for Casper – like the flag and mug races – but I'm also happy to try other things as long as it's safe for Casper and me. Today I've also put out some barrels and a giant horse ball and set up a slip rail – so it's going to be pretty wild!

Tackling obstacles like these is really good for building trust with your pony and for desensitising them to objects they may be wary of, such as traffic cones. It also helps with your balance as a rider – so while you may think it's all fun and games, there are plenty of benefits, too.

Mug mayhem

This is a fun game that is often used in mounted games. You have to pick up a mug from the first post and put it on the next one. You don't need to have fancy mounted games posts like these, but it is important that you use a metal mug. This won't smash like a ceramic or china mug, or shatter like a plastic one if your pony accidentally treads on it.

The mug makes a chiming sound when you hit it on the side of the post, which your pony may not be expecting, so if your pony is sensitive to noise, you might want to get him used to the sound from the ground before you try it in the saddle. I find it's best to pick up the mug from the bottom, not the handle, as this makes it much easier to put down on the next pole. Once you've got the hang of it in walk, give it a try in trot or even canter!

Brilliant barrels

I loved my time riding in the USA a few years ago and one of the most amazing things I did was barrel racing. It's an incredible balance of speed and tight turns and the horses love it. The aim is to ride around the barrels in a clover shape. As I start the barrel section of my obstacle course, I pop Casper into canter. I can feel him getting super-excited and quite speedy! As soon as we start to go around the first barrel, I look up and ahead to the next one – this helps us get a neat, tight turn. As we cross our tracks and switch from the right to the left bend, Casper re-balances himself with a flying change. Don't worry if your pony doesn't do flying changes, as you can change canter leads through trot. We turn tightly around the second barrel and then head to the third. It's another turn to the left before we're heading back to the start and finish line as quickly as we can.

Fun flags

You'll find all kinds of variations of flag races at gymkhanas and mounted games competitions, but essentially you'll need to be able to pick up a flag from one cone and put it into another. Some horses can be a bit frightened by flags blowing in the breeze, but it's great to slowly introduce them to your pony in case they come across similar things when you're out hacking. Have a go in walk to begin with and if you find that easy, why not try a trot or a canter?

Stepping stones

To complete the stepping stones you'll need to dismount from your pony and lead him alongside the stepping stones while you balance on them. Once you've finished all the steps, you'll need to get back on, but if you fall off one of the steps, you'll have to go back to the start and try again. If you don't have stepping stones like these, you could draw circles in the sand school for you to tread on instead. If you want to take this challenge to the next level, try to vault back onto your pony!

Bucket and beanbag

This simple game is all about accuracy. You need to collect a beanbag from one place and then drop it into a bucket. There's no fancy equipment required for this one. I've placed the beanbags on one of the barrels, but you could easily put them on a fence post or a jump block – whatever you have to hand. It's easy to make beanbags yourself by sewing together a square of fabric and filling it with dried beans. It's best to have three or four bags so that you can have a few goes without having to get off and pick them all up.

Collecting the beanbag is the easy part – what's tricky is dropping it into the bucket at speed but, as with everything, practice makes perfect!

Pace yourself

No matter whether I've tackled these challenges in walk, trot or canter, it's important that you go at the pace that feels right for you and your pony. If you're going too fast, the obstacles will feel impossible. It's better to be slow and steady than rush everything and feel that you aren't doing a great job.

On course

Once you've practised all the elements of your obstacle course, why not see if you can put them all together like I have? You could challenge yourself by timing how long it takes you to complete your course and then trying to beat your own course record the next time you ride. It takes a lot of effort to set up all the obstacles, so if you're able to leave them out for a few days, you can really make the most of it – and you'll see a huge improvement in your accuracy and your pony's confidence. All four of my equines like having a go at various bits of the course – Duke and Mickey in hand and Joey and Casper being ridden.

WINTER

EXTREME
WEATHER ROUTINE

*As soon as a weather warning is put in place,
I leap into action*

HIGH WINDS CHECKLIST

Ahead of time
- charge torch batteries in case of a power cut
- lay the jump wings on the ground so they aren't blown over and broken
- put extra bedding in the horses' stables

On the day
- bring the horses into their stables
- feed plenty of haylage to keep them happy and occupied
- check how much water the horses are drinking and give them a mash if I'm worried they aren't drinking enough
- put the radio on for Joey to keep him calm

After the storm
- look for fallen trees
- check the fencing is secure before the horses go back out

Top tip
always keep at least a week's worth of forage and bedding for my animals in case we are cut off by bad weather.

FLOODING CHECKLIST

Ahead of time
- make sure feed, haylage and bedding is off the ground on pallets
- place sandbags across doorways if I have them
- move the donkeys to high ground or into their shelter

On the day
- turn the horses out if possible and use waterproof rugs if needed
- fork up bedding into one corner of the stable to try to prevent it getting wet.
- keep the horses away from fast-flowing rivers or ones likely to burst their banks
- make sure horses have access to forage – tying haynets to fences or trees if necessary

When the water subsides
- sweep away any remaining puddles
- clear out wet bedding and replace with dry
- check tack and feed rooms for water damage

58

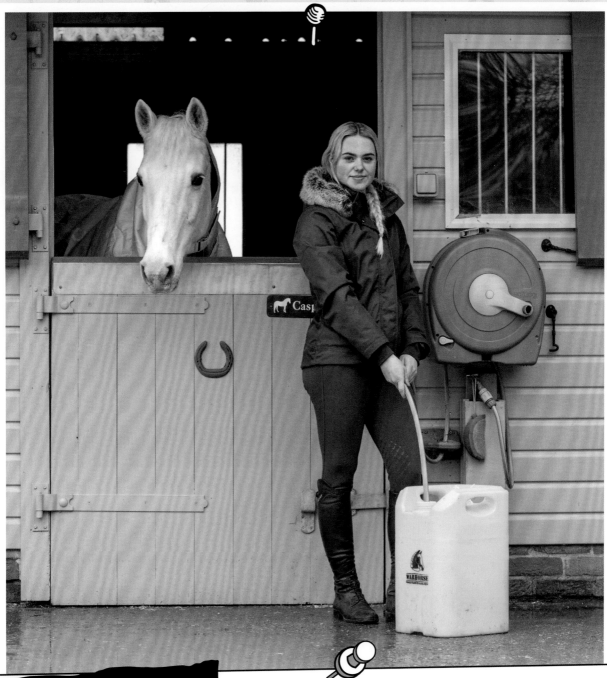

FREEZING TEMPERATURES CHECKLIST

Ahead of time
- fill water containers in case the taps freeze
- add lagging to pipes and taps to prevent them freezing
- fill the salt bin with grit

On the day
- break and remove ice from water troughs and buckets
- spread salt on the yard to help melt any ice that's formed or snow that's fallen

- make sure the horses are wearing the right weight of rug to keep them warm (although unclipped, healthy horses like Duke may not need rugging)
- keep the horses in if the ground is uneven, rutted and frozen solid, as they could injure themselves stepping in a frozen pothole
- feed hay to horses who are turned out to avoid them eating frozen or snow-covered grass, as that can bring on laminitis
- encourage the horses to drink by offering warm water if they aren't drinking as much as usual
- use a snow shovel to clear snow from the yard and to avoid flooding when it thaws

When things thaw
- check for burst pipes
- put the horses back out in their fields

Four seasons of MATCHY-MATCHY

As you know, I can't get enough matchy-matchy for my horses! Want to dress to impress all year round? Here's my colour guide by season...

SPRING FORWARD

In springtime, I absolutely love to dress up in pastel, floral colours that are fresh like the season! I try to go for pale blues, turquoise and lilac.

SUMMER LOVIN'

My favourite season! Summer is a time to go bright and bold, so don't hold back! Why not try out sunny yellows, vivid orange and bright pinks?

AUTUMN LEAVES

In autumn, it's all about earthy tones that match the crunchy leaves that are falling from the trees! Think green, burgundy and brown hues.

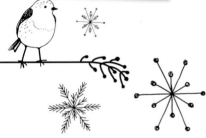

WINTER WARMERS

Winter tones are so beautiful! Stand out against frosty fields and snowy skies with rich navy, purples and reds, or embrace the cold with icy blues and greys!

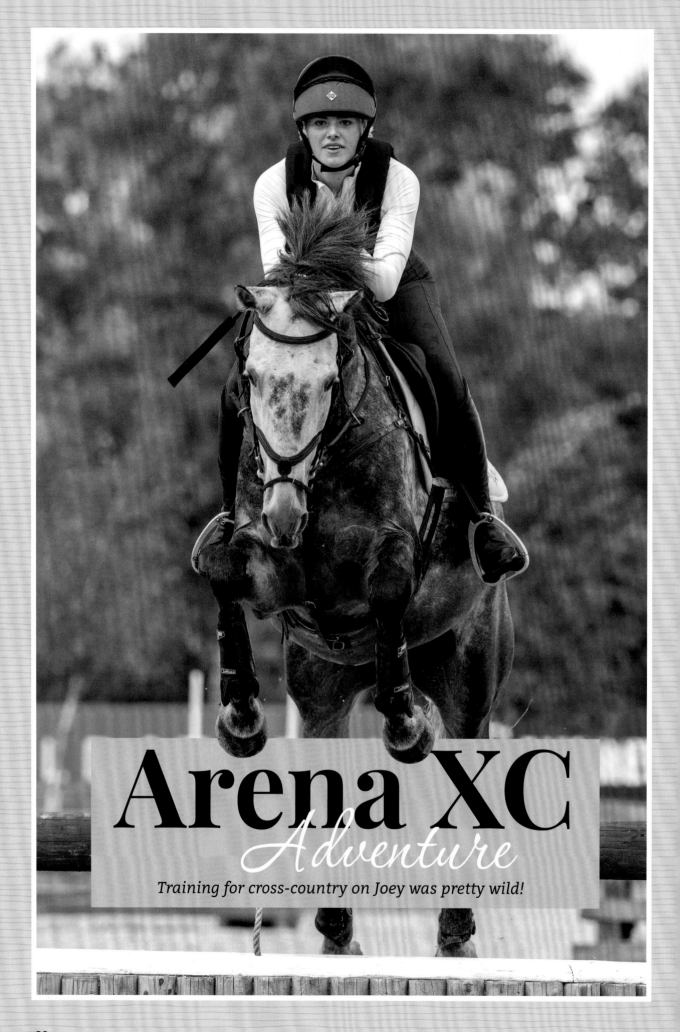

Arena XC
Adventure

Training for cross-country on Joey was pretty wild!

Perfect prep

I haven't done much cross-country riding with Joey but I think he absolutely loves it – to the point he gets so excited he can forget to concentrate on what we're doing. I keep this in the back of my mind when I'm warming him up and ask for loads of transitions within the pace and from one pace to another so that I know he's really listening to me. Because cross-country riding is fast paced, I make sure Joey is completely warmed up and ready to go before we start jumping.

Starting small

When you're at a schooling facility like this one, there will be all sorts of fences of varying heights and difficulty. I like to choose a simple fence which is lower than the height Joey and I normally jump to give us both a confident start. Even though it's a fairly small jump for Joey, I try my best to ride a good line to the fence and give him plenty of encouragement. Once we've jumped it a couple of times and I'm happy Joey is listening to me, it's time to explore the course.

Brilliant brushes

Brush fences like these are inviting to your horse because the brush will flex and bend if your horse's hooves go through it. As a rider, you can get caught out at a brush fence if you're expecting your pony to just skim through the top and he takes a great leap right over it instead! Fortunately for me, Joey takes it all in his stride and there are no giant leaps.

Super skinnies

Narrow fences are often called skinnies and they are becoming more and more popular and influential on cross-country courses. These fences test your accuracy and control, as they are much narrower than normal fences, making it easier for your horse to run out to one side. When I ride them on Joey, I aim for the very centre. making sure I have a good connection with my reins and that my legs are channelling him straight over the fence. Even though cross-country is ridden at quite a fast pace, I bring Joey back to a much steadier canter for narrow fences like this one to give me more time to make sure we're super-straight and so I can correct our line if I need to.

Ditch dilemas

Even though ditches are effectively a hole in the ground, some horses take a massive leap over them. With thousands of years of evolution telling them to be careful in case there's a crocodile hiding in there ready to leap out and snap them in its mighty jaws, it's not surprising some horses like to give them a wide berth altogether!

To give Joey time to assess the situation and work out what I'm asking him to do, I come back to a trot on the approach to our first ditch and give Joey lots of encouragement. I let him have his head so that he can lower his nose and take a look at the ditch to see for himself how harmless it really is and I sit up ready to fold forward as he takes off. Even though I can feel Joey is a little unsure, he listens to me and pops over the ditch first time. The next time I approached it, he was hopping over it like a pro!

Simple steps

This pair of drop fences are perfect for building Joey's confidence, as they're small and inviting, and are positioned on the way back into the main arena, which is really encouraging for a young horse. Again, I come back to a trot so that we're in control and set Joey up to gently hop off the first step, then the second. Unlike other fences, I sit very upright in the saddle and lean back slightly as Joey steps down so that my weight stays balanced in the saddle and I don't tip forward onto his shoulders.

Top tip

Whenever you ride cross-country – even if it's in an arena – you must wear an approved safety helmet and body protector.

Tricky lines

Riding cross-country isn't all about jumping over huge fences at the gallop – there are lots of tricky combinations to tackle as well. Here I'm jumping a triple of offset brush fences and there are a couple of options for tackling them. I've chosen to ride a straight line over all three elements. It means I have to be very accurate and jump the left-hand side of the first element, the middle of the second element and the right-hand side of the final part. Joey isn't a horse who tends to try to run out to one side, so this line works well for us and the distance between the elements is a good fit for Joey's stride length. If I were riding a longer-striding horse, I might take the diagonal route, which involves jumping the middle of each element on an angle.

All things ESME

Are you a true This Esme superfan? Take my quiz to find out!

I'm so lucky to have so many amazing fans who watch all my videos! But there are a few who stand out from the crowd because of their awesome knowledge of my channel. I've constructed this quiz to see how much you know and whether you're my ultimate super-fan! Good luck.

1 First things first, when did I start my YouTube channel?

a) 2020 ☐
b) 2017 ☐
c) 2015 ☐

2 I've posted over 750 videos on my channel so far, but do you know which one has the most views to date?

a) Tack Up With Me For A Show | Go Pro | This Esme ☐
b) Morning Routine Of An Equestrian | Summer 2018 | This Esme ☐
c) My Horse Riding Story | This Esme ☐

3 You guys have loved my *Challenge Esme* video series, but which of these activities have I NOT tried?

a) Horse archery ☐
b) Vaulting ☐
c) Riding a racehorse ☐

4 My brother has appeared in some of my videos over the years, but do you know his name?

a) Mike ☐
b) Mark ☐
c) Max ☐

5 I've been lucky enough to meet some amazing equestrians in my life. Do you remember which five-star eventer gave me a lesson on Joey in 2022?

a) Laura Collett ☐
b) Felicity Collins ☐
c) Bubby Upton ☐

6 One of my biggest adventures ever was when I went on a horseback safari! Which African country did I visit?

a) Botswana ☐
b) Zambia ☐
c) Kenya ☐

7 During lockdown, I challenged all three of my ponies to a tri-pony tournament! Who came out on top?

a) Joey ☐
b) Casper ☐
c) Mickey ☐

8 Finally, let's take a trip down memory lane. In a recent podcast episode, where did I say I worked before I became a full-time YouTuber?

a) A veterinary practice ☐
b) A pet shop ☐
c) A hair salon ☐

RESULTS

0-3 Fledgling fan
Looks like you need to watch some more of my videos before you reach superfan status! Why not take a look at some of my newest videos to learn more about me and my ponies? And I have a brand-new podcast you can check out, too, to find out all about my life!

4-6 Esme enthusiast
Not bad! You know some things about my channel, but there's still room for improvement. Why not comb through some of my past yearbooks and articles in PONY mag to get to know me even better? Not to mention, you'll pick up some top riding and pony care tips along the way!

7-8 Ultimate superfan
Wow! You know everything there is to know about me and my channel. From my horseback holidays to my daily vlogs, you really know your stuff. I couldn't ask for a more dedicated fan. Well done!

Answers: 1. C, 2. A, 3. C, 4. C, 5. B, 6. A, 7. B, 8. A

ALL IN
good time

Learn my top time-saving tips for when I'm at the yard

Running a yard of four horses is the best fun ever, but it certainly comes with some challenges! It takes a lot of time and effort to make sure everyone's properly cared for and that the yard stays tidy and efficient at all times. I have to be super-selective about my time because I only have so much of it to go around! That's why I try to shave seconds off my daily routine wherever I can with some handy time-saving tips that you can use as well. Here are some of my favourites!

Handy hanger

I try to reduce the number of trips I make to and from the tack room by ensuring I retrieve all my equipment in one go. Did you know you can use your whip as a portable clothes hanger? Simply slide it between the shoulders of your body protector and your helmet strap so you can carry everything with one hand, leaving your other arm free to carry your saddle and bridle.

Perfect prep

If you're like me and your alarm goes of super-early, you don't want to waste valuable seconds having to make mundane decisions! Give your future self a head start by laying out tomorrow's clothes the night before so you can get dressed in seconds. You can also pack your bag ahead of time and leave any items you'll need by the front door so you aren't panicking in the morning – it's a total gamechanger!

Delight in decluttering

Keeping your yard tidy and minimal will make your life so much easier! Having to sieve through items you no longer use in your grooming box and wading through rugs that no longer fit will only slow you down. Take time to declutter your space regularly by selling or donating items you don't use any more and invest in just a few high-quality products instead.

Water bucket wisdom

In the mornings when I'm mucking out, I don't have time to be walking up and down the yard filling water buckets. Instead of having to carry heavy buckets to and from the stables, I empty them out, put them back in position and use the long hose extension to refill each one. That way, it saves my back and gives me more time to get on with other jobs as I set a timer while they are filling so I remember to switch over to the next bucket and not let it overflow!

Haynet heaven

One of the most time-consuming jobs on the yard has to be filling haynets! And for me with four sets to make each day, it can take even longer! Luckily, I have a mega-useful hack that makes the job so much easier. Simply upcycle an old water bucket that's broken or has a hole in it by opening your haynet, placing it inside and wrapping the ends around the edges of the bucket. That way, you can quickly pop the hay inside and neatly close it with the string. No more struggling!

Organise your space

Who has time to go rummaging around for yard tools? No one! Why not place the items you use regularly in the locations you use them so they're to hand when you need them? For example, hang up your hoof pick by your pony's stable, leave the mucking out tools you use the most by the tack room door. Organise your rugs so the ones you'll use most this season are at the top of the pile. This will help streamline your yard and make everything run smoothly!

Batch it out

During the week, it can save you tons of time if you prepare everyday items in bulk. On a day when you're less busy, take the time to make up all the haynets and feeds your ponies will need that week so you can grab them and go. Pile haynets on top of each other so they're to hand straight away and you can store each pre-made feed in plastic boxes so you can quickly empty them out into buckets and soak them when needed. This will save you so much time when you're in a hurry!

Better out than in

When my horses are out for the day and I want to bring one of them in to ride or groom, instead of putting them in their stable, I prefer to tie them up outside or in the wash bay. That way, I can do what I need to without them messing up their beds and I don't then have to spend more time cleaning up again after such a short period of time! My ponies are more than happy to stand in the sun with a haynet while I tack up.

Reliable routines

When you're short of time, it's key to have a routine you can stick to. For example, I like to batch tasks together, so I'll do all four water buckets, then all four haynets, then muck out all the stables in the same order every day. That way, I can work on autopilot and get all the jobs done in one go, which is much quicker. I also time myself so I know exactly how long everything takes and I can make sure I leave enough time to get each task completed.

Bigger the better

One of my most beloved yard tools is my monster-sized broom! Making sure you have a good-quality yard broom will help you shave minutes off your morning routine. With just a few big sweeps, you'll have a clean yard in no time, rather than spending ages clearing every little bit with a tiny brush. Trust me, you won't look back!

HORSE-IFY
YOUR HOME

I've become obsessed with little details that make my cottage feel special to me. This tealight holder is a great example of how you can bring your horsey life into your home one and it was so easy to assemble, too.

Look out for a traditional stirrup iron – this one was actually an old one of my own, but you can often buy them cheaply on Marketplace or from an equine second-hand sale. Place a tealight holder on the stirrup tread and *voila*! You've made your very own horsey home accessory!

SUMMER EXTREME WEATHER ROUTINE

We all love summer, but sometimes it's too much for me and the horses

SUNBURN CHECKLIST

Ahead of time

- stock up on sun cream with a high SPF factor that is suitable for horses
- if your pony is particularly prone to sunburn, invest in a fly rug which has a high SPF factor
- make sure your pony has access to shady areas during the hottest part of the day and when the sun's rays are strongest

On sunny days

- apply sun cream to pink skin and areas that are prone to burning. Mickey hates this - but with his pink skin pigmentation, it's so important that he wears it
- think about whether it might be better to put your pony out in his field at night and in his stable during the day so that he has lots of shade to keep him cool and prevent sunburn

Top tip

Mickey's fly rug may look wild but the zebra stripes reduce the number of flies bothering him.

DROUGHT CHECKLIST

Ahead of time

If you know a drought is on its way, there are a few things you can do to be prepared such as...

- order in extra haylage or hay so that you can supplement your pony's diet if there isn't enough grass in his paddock
- restrict grazing to save the grass you have. Some people do this by making sure their horse or pony comes into their stable for at least four hours in every 24-hour period – making sure they have hay or haylage available during this time

If it happens

- hosepipe bans may be put in place. In this case, you will still be able to use a hose for essential cleaning, maintenance and the general wellbeing of horses and ponies. This means you can still use them to fill up water troughs and buckets for ponies to drink from and to clean any wounds
- make sure your pony is getting enough to eat. We're so used to worrying about ponies having too much grass that it seems strange to think of them not having enough. But, during periods of low or no rainfall, the grass stops growing and you may find you need to put haynets out in the field
- think about your pony's hooves. When we have a drought, the ground can become hard, which isn't good for fast work or jumping on. Dry conditions can also dry out your pony's hooves leaving them brittle. Hoof moisturisers can be applied daily to help with this

EXTREME HEAT CHECKLIST

Ahead of time

- keep an eye on the weather forecast for your area. Look out for temperatures in the high 20s and low 30s, as they may make your pony uncomfortably hot
- think about clipping your pony if he struggles with the heat

On the day

- keep your pony in the coolest place available for the hottest part of the day. For my horses, this means being in their stables
- if you're going to ride, make sure you choose the coolest part of the day. When it's hot, I ride first thing in the morning and stick to shady paths
- don't travel your pony unless it's an emergency and make sure the lorry windows are open. If you have a fan in your horsebox, make sure it's turned on
- use a sponge and cold water to help cool your pony down
- check your pony has access to fresh water at all times and if you are worried he's becoming dehydrated, speak to your vet

Casper's
FUN WITH POLES
Spicing up Casper's schooling sessions

Simple solution

If you don't have six poles, you can set this exercise up with just four as the side poles don't come into use.

Why I do poles

If Casper could choose what he does every day, he'd probably say jumping, jumping and more jumping! He just loves it – but it wouldn't be great for his joints, so I have to mix things up for him. Polework is a great way of doing that, and it has a lower impact on his joints than jumping – although it's still hard work, so not something he should do *every* day!

Ready to go

Before I tackle complicated lines of poles on Casper, I need to give him a good warm up. To do this, I either take him for a short hack or I walk him around the arena a few times on a long rein to let him loosen up. I try not to let him dawdle along – instead, I ask him to march forward so I know he's listening to me. Next, I ask for a trot and will ride plenty of changes of direction and transitions before we have a canter on each rein. Now we're all set!

Route one

This exercise goes straight down the middle of my layout. As I approach, instead of aiming for the middle of the first pole, I need to aim for the middle of the whole set up. This way, Casper can trot easily over the four poles that intersect the centre of the layout. He loves poles, so I only need to concentrate on our straightness and rhythm.

Two step

The next line I ride with Casper sees us heading over just the two poles to the side of the centre. It's a good test of whether he's listening to me, as we need to be very accurate to fit down this narrow channel. In trot Casper will do two trot steps between the poles – so it will be the same leg which leads over both poles. I ride this line in both directions and on both sides of the layout.

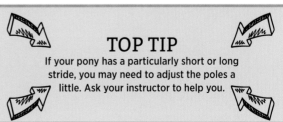

TOP TIP

If your pony has a particularly short or long stride, you may need to adjust the poles a little. Ask your instructor to help you.

MAKE A HORSEY
TEA TRAY

I love taking time out for tea with this cute horsey tray

WHAT YOU'LL NEED:

- a box tray
- two horseshoes
- wire brush
- horsey decorations or stencils
- brightly coloured paint
- strong adhesive or some screws
- PVA glue

1 Give your horseshoes a really good clean with a wire brush and ask an adult to remove any remaining nails. If your horseshoes have stud holes or nail holes near the ends, put screws through them to attach them onto your tray. Otherwise, a really strong adhesive such as *No More Nails* will do the job – but ask an adult to help you with this.

2 It's time to get creative! I found these super-cute wooden rocking-horse decorations in a craft shop, but you can use anything you like. Using red paint, I carefully coated each one and left them to dry.

3 Using PVA glue, I stuck the wooden rocking horses to my tea tray – being careful to space them equally along the long side of the tray.

Top tip

Only carry your tea tray by the horseshoe handles if you're sure they are screwed on tight. Otherwise, use the built-in handles – especially when carrying hot drinks.

Don't be put off by the name of this exercise – it's actually very simple and anyone can ride it. In fact, when I was younger I would call it an ice-cream cone when I was learning my dressage tests. Demi volte is a French phrase and it means half turn – or half circle.

HOW TO RIDE...
A Demi Volte

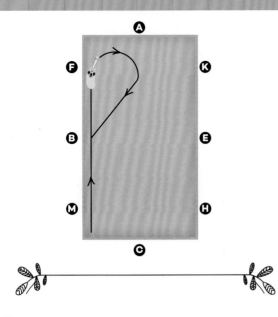

The start

To begin this movement, ride down the long side of the arena on the track. When I do this on Joey, I'm concentrating on two things – whether Joey is listening to me and where I need to start my turn. Once I've got my eye in for where the turn starts, I immediately look to the point where the half circle needs to finish.

The middle

I ask Joey to leave the track and ride an arc. Often this movement is ridden as a 10-metre half circle that will end on the centre line, but it can also be ridden as an 8-metre half circle or even a 6-metre one. During this part of the movement, I'm concentrating on Joey's inside bend and making sure that he's bent evenly from his nose to his tail.

The end

As we approach the end of our half circle, I look to the point where I want to rejoin the track. This could be the middle marker or the corner marker – and sometimes, in a test, it can be between the two. Unlike the shallow loop movement, Joey should be travelling straight as he comes back across the arena towards the track – then I ask him for inside bend as we join the track.

Top tip

This movement can also be used in preparation for counter-canter. The horse canters down the long side of the arena in true canter, makes a half circle to the inside before heading back to the track in a counter-canter.

BABY STEPS

I can't believe Duke is three already! Check out his goals and find out how far he's come in his very own baby pony tracker!

TASK	STATUS

Leading in hand
This is one of the most basic skills a horse or pony needs, but it's so important that they listen to you and respect your space.

> > > Good >

Being tied up on the yard
This isn't a natural situation for a horse, but learning how to stand on the yard will help horses when it comes to being seen by the farrier or vet, and when you want to groom or tack them up.

> > Fair > >

Hoof picking
Ever heard the saying no foot, no horse? Well, picking out your pony's feet twice a day is the most important part of good hoof care so it's essential all ponies master this.

> > Fair > >

Being touched on the head and ears
Horses can be sensitive about sudden movements around their head and ears, but in order to wear a headcollar or bridle you need to overcome this.

> > > > Excellent

Grooming
Not only is grooming an important part of caring for your pony – it's a great way to bond with them, too.

> > > > Excellent

Bathing
An essential task if you're thinking of heading to a show, but it's also important that you're able to wash your horse in case they get a skin condition or injury which requires cleaning.

> Needs practise > > > >

Accepting a bit and bridle
Wearing a bridle isn't something that should happen overnight. The process starts by gently massaging the muzzle and lips until the horse becomes comfortable opening his mouth when asked.

Not started > > > > >

Stepping back
It's good manners for a horse to step back from the stable door when asked. It reduces the chance of them escaping when you nip in to give them their dinner, too!

> > Fair > >

Being caught easily
Trying to catch a pony who won't be caught is one of the most frustrating things – but it's vital they learn to be caught in case they ever need the vet.

> > > > Excellent

GOALS

Duke is pretty good at being led in hand, but he can be a little cheeky when my mum looks after him, so Duke's goal in this area is to be comfortable being handled by all sorts of different people.

When Duke has a haynet, he's pretty relaxed about being tied up on the yard. However... when he hasn't got anything to eat he gets bored so quickly! This isn't unusual at his age, so our plan is to slowly increase the length of time he spends on the yard.

World Horse Welfare did a great job of Duke's initial training. For him to get 10/10, Duke's hoof care goal is to be just as good when the weather is wild and windy as he is the rest of the time.

This is an area Duke excels in! He absolutely loves having his ears scratched and is always sticking his nose in everything!

Being the fluffiest pony on the yard, Duke really likes a good pamper sesh. He will honestly stand for ages if I've got a brush in my hand.

This isn't Duke's favourite thing to do, so the first task is for him to accept being sponged on his hooves and lower legs, then small areas of his neck and the rest of his body. Eventually I will introduce the hose pipe – again starting with his feet and working my way up!

As Duke is only three years old, this isn't something I've tried with him. However, it's on our to-do list for the coming months, so watch this space!

I'm always strict with Duke when it comes to feed time and asking him to move back from the stable door as I enter. It was one of the things WHW talked about when I took Duke on as it's so easy for a little pony who's been hand-reared to try and be the boss.

Duke loves people, so he's always first to the gate when I go and get the boys in.

A DAY IN THE LIFE OF
Mickey

He may be retired, but he'll always be a legend to me

A DAY IN
THE LIFE

7.00 AM

The day starts with a quick cuddle and then breakfast served in Mickey's baby-blue bowl. Even though Mickey is the most vocal horse when it comes to feed time, he's fed third, as that's his place in the pecking order. I always check that he's eaten every last scrap of his feed, as it contains the medication he needs for his PPID (pituitary pars intermedia dysfunction).

I CAN HEAR MICKEY A MILE AWAY!

7.30 AM

After breakfast Mickey likes to head out into his field and the first thing he does each day is have a good old roll in the mud. As Mickey is an older horse who isn't ridden, this is a good time for me to check on his mobility – making sure that he's sound and isn't struggling to get up after his roll.

12 NOON

Although I don't do much with Mickey now he's retired, he packs a lot into each day including...
- grooming Duke
- being groomed by Duke
- eating grass
- foraging for exciting food in the hedgerow
- sleeping while standing up
- having a few more rolls and maybe even a lie down

4.00 PM

It's time for me to bring in Mickey and Duke from their paddock. I tie Mickey up on the yard and the first thing I do is pick out his feet into the skip bucket. This is another good opportunity to check how he's feeling. If Mickey becomes reluctant to pick up a hoof, it will generally mean that the leg he's left standing on isn't feeling 100%. If I notice changes like this, it's time to call the vet to ask them to examine him for things such as arthritic changes or laminitis that could impact on an older pony with PPID such as Mickey.

Next it's time for a spot of grooming and Mickey's favourite thing of all – scratchies! Mickey loves it when I scratch him at the base of his neck and by his wither. Sometimes he even curls up his top lip when I've found the perfect spot.

HOOF PICKING CAN TELL YOU A LOT

4.30 PM

Mickey heads to his stable. Even though he always has haylage available, you will normally find him standing at the back of his stable having a little snooze before it's time for his dinner.

6.00 PM

It's another of Mickey's favourite times... dinner time! He always whickers to me when I give him his bucket feed and I can't resist another cuddle. Later on, my dad will give him one last check and say goodnight.

WHERE THE
magic
HAPPENS

Come with me on a tour of my recording studio!

Filming YouTube videos isn't just about playing with ponies all day! There's also a lot of hard work that goes into planning, editing and social media scheduling. Come with me to see how I work behind the scenes in an exclusive tour of my studio!

Podcast passion

I've really enjoyed starting up my brand-new podcast *Esme's Country Life*! It's something I've been wanting to do for a while because I love listening to podcasts myself, and I thought it'd be a fun way to chat with you and update you on how my life's going. I've set up an area in my studio where I keep my microphone on a stand so I can have my hands free while I'm talking, and I've stuck special foam all over the ceiling to make sure it sounds great, too.

Careful editing

Even though it can be time consuming, editing my content can actually be pretty creative and fun! I use special editing software to ensure my vlogs are absolutely perfect and professional, and I make sure I edit out any mistakes or bloopers along the way! I often listen to the audio through a pair of headphones so I can get the full effect, and I have a big display screen so I don't miss any detail. Anyone can learn to edit videos and make eye-catching thumbnails for YouTube – it just takes practice!

Did you know?

My lovely new office is actually my old loft. It's right above the studio and I can see the horses from the door. It's the perfect space for me.

Social media savvy

As you know, I try to stay active across all my social media platforms, including Instagram, Facebook and TikTok. I capture content throughout my day-to-day life, so I always have something new and fun to post. When I can, I like to plan my content calendar ahead of time so I don't have to worry about posting every single day. To do this, I use a social media scheduling tool from my computer. It's super-easy to do, but it does require some forward planning!

Little accomplishments

I try to put some time aside each day to deal with smaller tasks that I need to complete when I'm in my office. This includes things like replying to emails, liaising with my brand sponsors and planning my week! I like to sit down with a cup of tea, pop on a podcast or some relaxing music and get to work. My office is a great place to knuckle down and get into some deep-focus work without too many distractions.

Top tip

Do you procrastinate when you have a long to-do list? I find it helps to break up your time into manageable chunks by setting a timer for just 20 minutes and trying to work the whole time. I often find that once I'm into the task, I want to keep going, even when the time's up!

Take a break

Of course, I can't work flat out all day long, so it's important that I have some downtime. I have a cosy corner in my studio where I can chill out with some snacks for 10 minutes or so to refresh my mind before I get back to the nitty-gritty.

Water

baby

I discovered Joey just loves water – and so do I!

Joey has always been a total mud monster and he's certainly not scared of splashing through a few puddles, but I have to admit I never knew he was so fearless when it came to water. Here's how we progressed from splashing around to jumping into water!

Confidence is key

Before you can even think about asking a pony to jump into water, you need to be sure that they are comfortable in water. With Joey I take every opportunity to ride through puddles when we see them, so he learns that going through water is no big deal. When I take him to the beach I ask him to walk along the water's edge so that he gets his feet wet and where it's safe to take him in a bit deeper, I ride him into the sea until he's about knee deep in the water.

On this cross-country training day I walked him through the water to begin with. Once he was happy I tried walking in, then trotting out. Before long, Joey was happy cantering through it – and soaking me in the process!

On dry land

The next step towards the goal of jumping into water is to jump a small fence that allows the horse to land on the dry, before heading into the water on the next stride. This little log I found was perfect. Even though Joey was feeling super-confident, I sat up tall on the approach and asked Joey for a collected canter so that I could ride him forwards if he became spooked by the water at the last second. Jo-Jo was a total star and jumped it beautifully before splashing through the water again.

One step at a time

We progressed to this tiny little step down, which I approached in walk so that Joey could see the water. I sat up and allowed him to lower his head and neck so that he could see the water below. Using my leg aids to encourage him, Joey gently stepped down and then trotted on through the water.

Leap of faith

Once Joey was happily popping off the little step and then going through the water, I asked him to approach it in trot. This time he leapt off the step – landing straight in the water with a giant splash! I can't believe how confident he was.

Ultimate challenge

Our final task at the water complex was to jump a fence in the middle of the water. This small log pile was ideal as the water on the approach was very shallow so the horses don't lose much momentum on the way in. Even though Joey seemed to be taking everything in his stride, I put my leg on as we entered the water to keep him in a forward canter and he popped the fence with ease. Mission accomplished!

Spring cleaning

My six steps to make your horsebox spick and span

Whether you have a horsebox or a trailer, it's super-satisfying to give it a proper deep clean so you can arrive at shows in style! I do this job about once a year. It's hard work, but I feel so happy when it's done. Here's the method I like to use to make my horsebox pristine from the inside out!

THIS ESME

Top tip

I try to wait for sunny day before cleaning the horsebox. That way, the inside will dry a lot quicker and you can leave the ramp and windows open for better air flow.

STEP 1 TIDY UP THE INSIDE

Remove all items from the horse area. Take down haynets and leadropes that have been left on board. Then, fork any bedding, hay or muck into your wheelbarrow to go onto the muck heap. Now you have a clear area to deep clean!

STEP 2 THE BIG SWEEP

Next, take a thick-bristled broom and give the horsebox floor a thorough sweep. Spend time removing loose debris from the mats and ramp, and clear any drainage holes in your horsebox floor. You can also use a duster or corn broom to dust the walls and windows and remove cobwebs. If you're allowed to use the vacuum cleaner, you'll find it's amazing at getting the last bits of dirt off the floor and ramp.

STEP 3 POWER WASH

The next thing I do is jet wash the horse area. I use a special attachment on the end of the hose that gives the water extra power so I can blast away any grime, mud and cobwebs. This is a really satisfying job and makes the horsebox look brand new again! I always find the wall where I hang up the haynet gets especially filthy, so I like to focus on that part the most. Remember to clean the partition, too!

STEP 4 THE BODY WORK

Now it's time to close the ramp and get cleaning the outside of the box. I stick with the pressure washer for this, but you could use a bucket and sponge or a mop for the difficult-to-reach areas. Make sure you focus on the wheel arches, wing mirrors and doors because this is where stubborn dirt can build up.

CLEAN

Top tip

If your horsebox or trailer has a groom's area or driver's area, don't leave that out! Use all the same tips to give every part a thorough spring clean. If it feels like too much in one go, why not aim to clean one area of the horsebox a day?

STEP 5 SOAP IT UP

After power washing the whole horsebox, I go in with a cloth, sponge and some car shampoo to give those hard-to-clean areas some extra attention. This is a great way to remove any extra-stubborn stains and make your horsebox glow! I pay close attention to the door handles, lights and windows.

SOAP

STEP 6 TIME TO DRY

Once I've cleaned the whole horsebox, it's time to pop the ramp back down to create an air flow so that the horsebox dries inside and out.

THIS ESME

Dream big

*Find out how you can achieve
your dreams, big or small!*

I've been really lucky to have achieved so much in my life over
the past few years, from growing my channel to buying my
very own cottage and, of course, keeping my four gorgeous
horses fit and healthy. If you have goals you want to reach just
like me, but aren't sure how to do it, then I've got some helpful
advice to help you achieve anything you put your mind to!

2015: Launching YouTube channel

2019: Travelling to Senegal with the Brooke Charity

2020: When I got the horse of my dreams

Top tip

When my mind feels
cluttered, I find it helpful to do
stream-of-consciousness writing.
This is when you write whatever
comes into your mind at the time
without giving it too much thought.
You'll be surprised what thoughts you
unlock! You can also do the same thing
by talking into a voice recorder on
your phone as if you're talking
to a trusted friend.

Your heart's desire

Have you ever felt a little lost? Are you
unsure which direction you want your
life to head in next? Well then, it's time
to have a good hard think about what
it is you really want. It can seem a little
daunting, but it's important to have a
clear vision of your goals so you can
make plans to action them! I find it really
helpful to get my thoughts down on
paper by writing in my journal. To help
you, try answering these journalling
prompts...

Visualise it

I love using my imagination and creativity to help bring my goals to life and you can, too! One of my favourite ways to focus my mind and get inspired is to create a vision board. You can do this by printing off or cutting out images and quotes that are related to your goals and use them to make a beautiful collage to hang on your wall. Spend time selecting images that mean something to you and that will help pick you up if you need a little extra motivation! Make sure you hang your vision board somewhere you'll always see it as a daily reminder of why you want to achieve your goals.

Top tip

You can flick through magazines, search online and use social media to help you find inspiring images that will look amazing on your vision board.

2023: I started my country life podcast

2022: When I bought my own cottage

SOLD

2021: Reached half a million subscribers

Ask yourself...

What makes me the most happy in my life right now?

....

....

What does my dream life look like?

....

....

What three short-term goals do I have?

....

....

What three long-term goals do I have?

....

....

What is the main thing that's holding me back from achieving my dreams?

....

....

Which of my goals means the most to me and why?

....

....

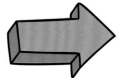

Step by step

When you're going after your goals, it's important to break each one down into manageable tasks so that you don't feel overwhelmed by them. Spend time thinking about actions you can take that will take you one step closer to where you want to be. I love planning, so I find it really useful to set myself targets across the year that I can then aim towards. For example, make a note of what you want to have achieved in a certain number of weeks or months from now – whether that's cantering confidently, tackling your first showjumping course or growing your social media channels. You'll get a huge sense of achievement when you make small wins and that will encourage you to keep going!

Top tip

Make sure you're realistic when setting yourself a timeframe. You don't want to knock your confidence, so it's important to allow yourself a practical amount of time to achieve each step.

Overcome setbacks

Sometimes things might not go to plan, but that's okay. After all, horses have their own thoughts and feelings that we can't control, which is all part of the fun! Even if you have a wobble in confidence, get stuck on something, or simply feel demotivated for a time, it's how you deal with these setbacks that matters most. Remind yourself why you wanted to achieve your goal in the first place. Don't lose sight of the bigger picture! That way, you'll stay determined and you'll keep trying until you get to where you want to be.

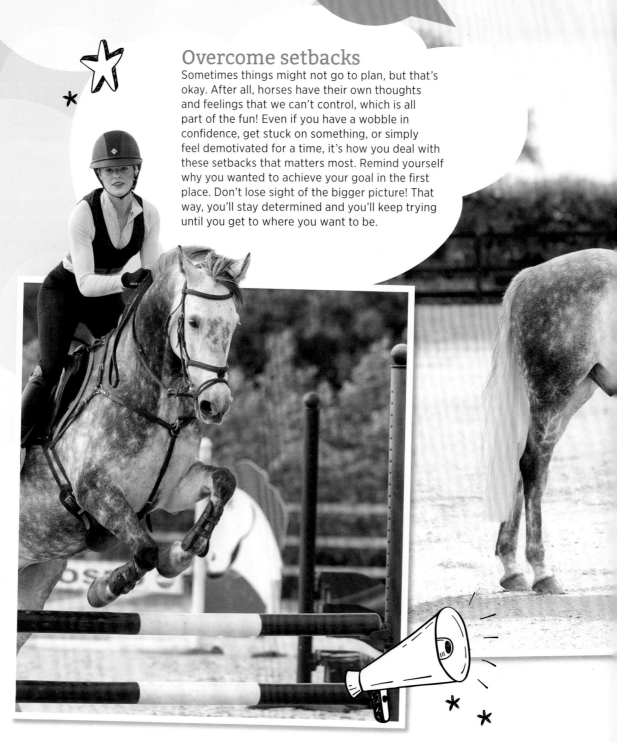

Stay on your own path

It's easy to compare yourself with others, especially in the equestrian world! While it can be helpful to be inspired by other riders, YouTubers and friends you look up to, try not to base your success on what other people have achieved. Everyone is on their own path and is going at their own pace. So even if you don't feel as good as someone else right now, focus on what you can do to improve rather than become jealous or unmotivated to carry on. Perseverance and self-belief are key!

Enjoy the journey

When striving for any goal, it's really important to live in the present and enjoy the journey, rather than rush towards the finish line! Revel in every small achievement along the way and, above all else, make sure you're having fun. That's why we do it, after all!

Top tip

If you need a little pick-me-up, why not ask a trusted friend or your instructor for support? Sometimes a few words of encouragement are all you need!

IF MICKEY TOOK OVER MY
TikTok

Naughty Mickey has got his hooves on my TikTok account again! What hilarious things has he posted this time?

"Livin' my best life"

Living my best life! Ain't no one gonna get me clean.
#Mud #MuddyPony #KeepOnRolling

"You're joking"

When Esme comes to collect me from the field without a treat.
#You'reJoking

"Wow that's awesome"

Overrated much!
#Overrated
#ICanDoItBetter

HIT THE ROAD

Make sure your pony's ready to set off with my ultimate travel kit list!

Top tip

If the weather's looking iffy, packing a rain sheet will help keep your pony clean and dry if he's tied outside in a shower, and you can use it to cover your tack while you're getting ready, too.

When travelling your pony in the horsebox or trailer, it's really important to make sure he's got everything he needs to be comfortable and safe. To help me prepare for every outing, I use this handy kit list to make sure my ponies have everything they need before we go. Let's check it out together!

Top tip

It's a good idea to use a poll guard to help protect your horse's head while travelling, especially in low-roof lorries and trailers.

Harmless headwear

What your pony wears on his head while travelling is really important. I like to travel Joey in a part leather headcollar because it's more likely to snap and release in an emergency than one made of nylon or webbing. I pair this with a breakaway trailer tie that I clip on when I load up. The quick-release action is the perfect choice when it comes to safety, so it's a must-have for any horsebox.

Prepared provisions

Most horses enjoy munching a haynet while they're on the move, so make sure you tie one for your pony to nibble on so he stays occupied during the journey. I often like to take a spare in the groom's area as well in case Joey runs out en route. That way, there'll be something for him to munch when he's standing waiting, too. I also never forget to take a container full of fresh water in case he gets thirsty, and, of course, lots of treats so he knows he's a good boy!

Total tail protection

I like to travel my ponies in tail guards because it helps protect their docks while in transit, as the dock is a delicate area of the tail. A guard also helps keep Joey's tail looking neat and clean if we're on our way to a competition. Many people like to use a traditional tail bandage, but I prefer to use a tail guard because it's quicker to put on and looks super-smart, too!

Cool coverings

It's a good idea to take any rugs your pony may need on your outing. A cooler rug is essential because he may get a little sweaty on the journey and having a thin rug to help wick away moisture will help keep him comfortable. It's especially useful to put one on for the journey home, because your pony may feel a little chilly after you've sponged him off to remove any sweat from being ridden!

Lavish leg wear

Protecting your pony's legs is one of the most important things to consider when travelling him. Whenever we go anywhere, I always travel Joey in a set of travel boots so I know his legs are completely covered. Other people prefer to use bandages and gamgee with hock and knee boots, but I prefer travel boots because they are quick, easy and fully protective! There are so many types you can buy, but it's up to you to decide which ones will be best for your horse – but be sure to choose the correct size for him.

MAKE A HORSEY
DOOR HANGER

Let everyone know what you're up to with this cute door hanger

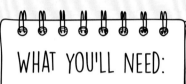

WHAT YOU'LL NEED:

- an offcut of wood
- two small screw eyes
- string
- scissors
- pencil
- paint or marker pens

1 Take your piece of wood and decide which way up you'd like it to hang. Then, screw in the screw eyes to the top of the wood – one on each side. You should be able to do this by hand, but ask an adult to help you.

2 Cut the string to size. It must be long enough to tie onto each screw eye and loop over whatever you plan to hang your door sign from. Now, carefully tie one end to each of the screw eyes.

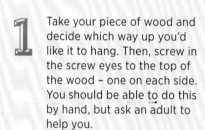

Top tip

If you are going out for a ride always make sure someone knows where you're going or use an app on your phone so they can track your progress.

3 Once you've planned what you'd like to say on your door hanger, write it carefully on the wood in pencil. This way you can erase it if you make a mistake. There are lots of slogans you might want to use like: *Gone riding, Do not disturb, Keep out, Horses welcome – people tolerated*, or choose something of your own!

4 Using paint or a marker pen, carefully go over your writing and leave to dry.

Gone Riding